The Power of Forgiveness

Healing Beyond my Wounds

Heidy Mejia

DEDICATION

First and foremost, I want to thank the Father, the Son, and the Holy Spirit because they have never forsaken me and are everything to me. I want to express my gratitude to my husband, Tony Mejía, for his support and dedication. Since I met him, he has been a blessing in my life. I also want to thank his children, whom I love as if they were my own, and have brought blessings to my life. I am more than grateful for my daughters, who have been present in every stage as I wrote parts of my testimony. Thank you for every effort, support, and love you have always shown me. Likewise, I want to thank Delmis Quiroz and his wife Agnelesse for their excellent work and commitment in every book cover. Last, but certainly not least, I am thankful to my pastors for always having a word from God that encourages us to keep going and for believing in restoration. I also express my gratitude to my in-laws, siblings, mother, and those friendships that become family and push us towards our goals.

To protect privacy, the names of all individuals mentioned in my testimony have been changed to avoid any form of recognition.

Table of Content

Prologue

Reading The Power of Forgiveness by my wife, Heidy Mejia, reveals the depth of wounds and how her love for God grew and helped her understand the need to heal and forgive. Often, we mistakenly believe that forgiving is solely for the benefit of the person who hurt us. However, this book emphasizes that forgiveness is truly for our own growth and well-being. This book shares a true-life story of how God showed Heidy that her wounds were holding her back from progressing in life. By letting go and moving forward, she experienced the best thing she could do for herself. Heidy is not only a great mother, wife, and friend, but also an inspiring example of personal growth. Witnessing her journey has been remarkable. I have no doubt that this book, along with her first book, Beyond My Wounds, will help you realize the importance of breaking free from chains and experiencing transformational change within yourself. Both books have impacted me in countless ways, and I pray that they have the same profound effect on you.
Tony Mejia

Forgiving My Father

Many of those who read my first book have asked me how I managed to forgive my father, among other questions. In this book, I will talk to you a little about the experiences I went through and how the process of forgiveness was. Forgiving is not a feeling, it is a decision that we must make, it is an attitude or action that we must put into practice. This decision must be made with firmness and determination. Forgiving involves giving up hatred and ill will towards those who hurt us, and praying for them so that they too can be released and healed.

If we remain focused on the pain and the harm caused, we will not be able to heal or be free. If you focus on the wound and the damage caused, you will continue to feel that pain and live filled with traumas and fears that bring painful consequences to your life. But if you focus on the lesson learned, you will gain experiences and tools to not only heal yourself, but also to help others heal and become a blessing to thousands of people through your story and testimony. A wounded person hurts others without realizing it; a healthy and restored person can help others get out of that place of pain and despair.

Forgiving doesn't necessarily mean exposing ourselves again to the same situations or people who led us to difficult experiences full of pain. For years, I lied to myself to hide the pain, shame, hatred, and many conflicting feelings that arose from so much abuse.

I loved my dad, but at the same time, I felt a bit of resentment towards him. Not only because of the abuse but also because my father was not present. When I got good grades, graduated from school, or just on my birthday, there was not a phone call; he only looked for me when it was convenient and always abused.

I couldn't understand how someone who was supposed to protect, guide, love, and take care of a girl could be the main cause of so much pain, so many wounds, and fears. And at the same time, that same person would open doors spiritually that would lead to similar stories repeating in my life. Forgiving was not easy; for a long time, I believed that I had forgiven my father because I didn't wish him harm and thought that was enough.

Complete healing in my life began when I wrote part of my testimony in my first book. I wrote that book many times and erased it. First, I wrote about everything I had gone through, and little by little, the Holy Spirit led me to relive the pain. In the process, I cried a lot, had to fast several times, and remain in prayer. As I wrote, I was being confronted with the reality that I had not fully healed or forgiven. I had to delete more than half of the first book because the Holy Spirit made me feel that the purpose was to restore, not to expose damaging the testimony of people who had marked and abused me, besides my father, was something I didn't want to do. The purpose has always been and continues to be to glorify God and talk about forgiveness and restoration.

In the process of forgiving properly, not just with words, I had a vision in which I was in a church, praying and seeking the presence of God. I could feel it, but I knew there was so much more than just having an experience or being touched by God during a service. I didn't want to settle for a half-hearted life in God. In the vision, I prayed and asked God to remove everything that hindered me. My father always came to mind, and as I prayed, I would say, "Touch everything, change everything in me, but not in that area with my father. Just completely erase it from my memory, I want to wake up one day as if it never happened, to have it never again in my memory." I told God that I had already forgiven him, but I didn't want to remember or talk about it. I prayed for years.

In that same vision, I sat on a church bench and looked towards the altar, where I saw my father. My body froze, and I started crying, asking, "What is he doing here after all the evil he has done to so many people?" I saw someone praying for him, but I could also see the demons that had bound and possessed him since my childhood. They looked at me and mocked me. In that moment, my father fled from the church, also possessed, and stared at me menacingly.

At that moment, I felt fear and deep pain. A tall man with bright clothes sat beside me. I couldn't see his face, but his presence embraced me and gave me peace. He placed his hand over mine and said, "You must forgive, I know it hurts, but give that to me, let me act in my way, not yours." I fell to my knees and surrendered everything, saying, "I don't want to continue like this. Go deep, teach me how to forgive and forget, how to love as your son Jesus."

From that day, I wanted to talk to my father, but I didn't know how. God used my pastors to guide and counsel me on how to spiritually renounce the things that bound me. So, I started working on areas of my life and surrendering them to God, making the necessary changes.

About a year passed, and I started writing my book again. It was nearly finished, ready for the revision and printing process. I had overcome that painful stage where I felt I fell into depression, and my body experienced so much pain while writing and reliving those moments.

I will translate your book into English:

One day, I was in my car with my daughters, waiting to enter a medical appointment. It was very early in the morning, and I closed my eyes. I was meditating and praying when suddenly I heard a loud but gentle voice. That voice said to me, "Heidy, have you forgiven your father?" I replied, saying, "Yes, I have forgiven him." The voice asked me, "Are you sure you have forgiven him?" I responded, "Yes, I am sure." Then, that authoritative voice said to me, "Then why don't you pray for him? Why do you feel afraid to speak with him and express what you have felt for years, to tell him that you forgive him and love him, and to wish for his repentance and freedom?" I said, "What if he doesn't change and causes even more pain in me?" The voice said to me, "Forgiveness liberates, heals, and restores. It breaks chains and sets you free and brings you closer to me." I replied, saying, "Then, give me the strength and put the words in my mouth."

I was deeply moved, and tears were flowing. I asked God for forgiveness because for so many years I had deceived myself by holding onto this pain and lack of forgiveness.

Suddenly, my phone rings; it was my father. My initial reaction was to reject the call. But quickly, I reflected on the experience I had just had. I also asked God for strength and called him back. He answered, we greeted each other, and he began to speak, and I understood that he had not changed nor repented. He made comments about my physical appearance, as he had seen pictures of me and my daughters through a family member. Then he asked me to send him pictures of one of my daughters, the one who resembles me the most, as she reminded him a lot of when I was young. Of course, I told him that I couldn't send him pictures because I wasn't comfortable with that.

My heart wanted to burst out of my chest and say so many things to him, but I understood that I had to show the love and mercy of God in me, and above all, forgive. I was able to contain myself and I began to talk to him about God...

I told him: I need you to listen to me.

You don't know what has become of my life because of the damage you caused me by abusing me and having had to witness how you abused my friends and stepsisters.

At a very young age I fell into the vice of drugs and became addicted, alcoholic. I have struggled with depression and many times I tried to take my life. I haven't managed to love a man and for years I couldn't love myself. I didn't have a father who hugged me when I felt fear, sadness, or loneliness. When my friends talked about their first sexual experience, it struggled in my mind not to be able to speak like them since you stole my innocence.

All the illusion of every girl getting married in white and getting to the altar by her father's hand, you stole it from me. For years I was an object and used by people who, like you, had to protect me and no one did anything to help me. Nobody sat down with me to tell me that I was special and had courage. You weren't there, and the few memories together with you have been full of pain, fear and doubts. I never understood why, why am I your daughter?

For years I struggled with all this, I didn't know that I had a right over my own body and that no one should abuse my physical, emotional, verbal or sexually. I let him know how not only the abuse of me in my childhood but also people who knew him and took care of me from the same church and other relatives of him abused me.

I told him how in my youth I was drugged and abused, I felt that it was something I was already destined for because of him. I couldn't have a normal childhood; my youth was difficult full of hatred and complexes. For years I didn't sleep well since I woke up with nightmares where men loved me and raped me.

The response from my father was something I never imagined and certainly painful. He said to me, "It was your mother's fault, she wasn't enough for me." At no point did he ask for forgiveness or show any empathy towards me. Nevertheless, I continued the conversation with him.

In this way, I forgave my mother. For years, I wondered why she never did anything, why even though relatives knew what was happening, no one did anything about it. This filled me with a lot of pain, but God healed that wound and I was able to forgive and understand that she was also a victim of him, just like me. I spoke to him about the love and mercy of God. How God healed my heart and set me free from addictions. God forgave all my sins even when I didn't deserve it, and I also forgave him. I told him that I needed to be free, to open his heart to God, who can break all the chains in his life. That God would give him eternal life and transform his life. That he should accept Him as his Savior and turn away from sin because God wants to change his life and heal all his wounds. He just must open his heart.

My father only responded, "Wow! You had never told me all of this. I hope your life gets better and tell my granddaughters that I would like to meet them." At the end of the conversation, I told him that I loved him despite everything and that I forgave him for everything. And if he ever changed and could respect me and see me as his daughter, then we could keep in touch. But regardless of his decision, I wanted him to know that I would always pray for him and that I loved him. I wished for him to find God and be free and saved. He replied, "Thank you," and ended the call.

Afterward, I began to cry and pray, asking God to have mercy on my father and transform his heart. The conversation was difficult but necessary because I felt like something broke and experienced peace. I felt free. For those who have asked if I still communicate with my father, I don't have direct communication with him, but I do through relatives.

Healing Releasing Forgiveness

Forgiving Alfredo (the young man who drugged me and abused me along with others) was something that took longer. I didn't know how to do it or what steps to take, since I had no way to contact him. I prayed and asked God to direct me and help heal and forgive him.

Every adverse situation or pain event brings with it consequences, it marks our lives in one way or another. Many leave mistrust, trauma, fears, emotional disorders, guilt and most leave a great void, among other things.

For example, my father's abuse marked me in the sense that I didn't learn to love myself or give myself courage. I lived with fears and the fear of abandonment due to the absence of my father in my life and that of my brothers. The lack of a father led me to fall into the hands of the wrong people looking to fill that void and trying to find that father figure. The traumas caused by Alfredo's abuse led me to use drugs to hide the pain. When Alfredo abused me, I was already a young woman and I understood more the seriousness of what happened. The hatred for men began to grow in me, I couldn't trust anyone. I became cold and indifferent. I was looking to fight, and I even got to self-harm because I felt hatred and disgust towards myself. I was filled with complexes and insecurities; I didn't believe in myself, and it was difficult for me to love myself.

Now I was facing my reality. I had to forgive and treat these areas of my life, such as the fear of loving, trusting, and committing myself. I had to heal areas in my life, but everything in me felt the need for him to also be free to forgive him.

While praying one day, he asked God for Alfredo, he asked him to touch his heart no matter where he was and to repent and turn away from all sin. I didn't know how to do it, I had no way to communicate with him, but I needed to forgive and close that chapter in my life.

I felt like praying and saying these words again and again out loud. "Alfredo, I forgive you, I declare freedom over your life in the powerful name of Jesus and I cancel and close every door. I declare myself free of everything that has bound me to you through that abuse." He repeated aloud as he prayed: "I forgive you, be free."

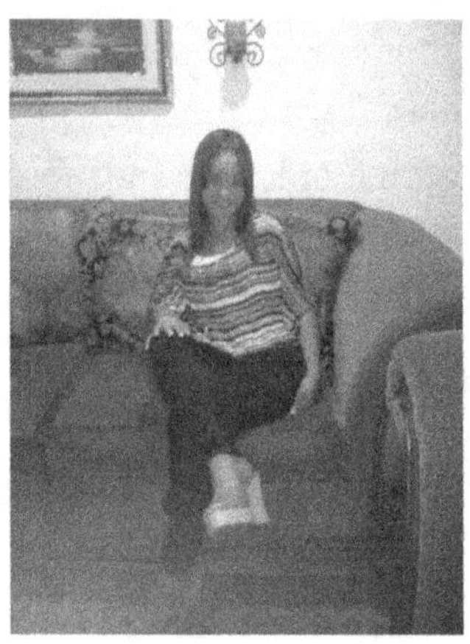

As I declared these words, I felt a supernatural and difficult to explain peace that filled my life. I knew that it was the presence of God doing the work and healing those wounds. From that day on, I can talk about what happened with Alfredo without feeling shame, hatred, or pain. I can freely pray for him so that he will be blessed and saved.

Liberation Through Forgiveness

Despite my life having significantly improved in every aspect, there was still something deep inside me. It hurt me, made me cry just by remembering it. It was a very intense feeling that was rooted in me. I couldn't understand how or why someone could cause so much pain, so much harm, not only to me but also to my daughters.

The abuse at the hands of Diego was one that marked my life in a different way. What I suffered before in my childhood and youth I overcame it more easily because I knew it hadn't been my fault. But with Diego I felt guilty, betrayed, and responsible for what my daughters still saw.

I was the one who accepted it in my life, and he took advantage not only by hurting me, but my daughters were victims and had to see the physical abuses that I suffered at the hands of this man.

That was difficult for me to forgive, not only him but also to forgive myself for opening that door that led us to painful situations. That's why it is necessary to heal and close chapters, overcome traumas, so as not to repeat the same story repeatedly. Every time I tried to pray for him, I couldn't, I would just start crying and ask God questions, among them, why so much suffering? Why so much abuse in my life? The pain was still there, as well as the shame and guilt.

Time passed and one day I sat down with one of my daughters to talk about a situation she was experiencing because of Diego and how seeing violence against her mother affected them. She said to me, "Mommy, let's pray and forgive him, so that even though he is in jail, he can be free from his sins and change. You have taught us that our struggle is against Satan, and he used Diego to complete the harm in your life and ours. She tells me: remember how he would call on Satan and invite him into his body before doing what he did. Let's forgive him and forget. God has been good, and you have always taught us to forgive."

I started crying, I hugged my daughter, and together we prayed for Alfredo, declaring forgiveness and restoration. Out loud, we declared forgiveness and that all spiritual doors were closed.

Days later, I received calls from the court and the prosecutor's office, telling me that Alfredo had confessed everything he had done and expressed remorse. Then I received a letter from him asking for our forgiveness. Through one of his family members, I let him know that we forgave him and that he should seek God.

We were able to forgive and overcome the things that came into our lives because of this abuse, such as the fear we felt just by hearing his name. Our hearts were healed and restored. We could see, once again, God's hand working in our favor.

Forgiving myself was the hardest part. I carried this feeling of guilt because I knew I had decided outside of God's will, which led me to drift away from Him and cause wounds and traumas in my life. My daughters have always expressed gratitude towards me and great admiration, but I felt this pain that they were victims because of my fault.

One day, they sat beside me to talk about how good God has been and to remember how many times His hand has protected us and lifted us up. I took that opportunity to ask for their forgiveness for all the damage caused. I explained to them how bad it is to make decisions outside of God's will. We hugged and prayed together. God restored us, and thanks to Him, we have always been very united, putting God first in our lives. It all starts with a decision that we must make and then put into action.

First Steps: Accept Your Condition

I would like to begin by explaining some traumas that arise from physical and sexual abuse. Some of them are:

1. Emotional trauma: feelings of fear, shame, guilt, anger, profound sadness, confusion, and lack of motivation to move forward.

2. Psychological trauma: mental health issues, post-traumatic stress disorder, anxiety, depression, and even eating disorders.

3. Sexual trauma: difficulty with intimacy, rejection of intimacy with your partner, low self-esteem, distrust in others and even in oneself. Your self-esteem is very low, and there may be confusion about your sexual orientation.

4. Interpersonal trauma: you find it difficult to establish healthy long-term relationships based on trust. You develop a mechanism of self-destruction and fail to learn how to set personal boundaries.

Each person faces different types of traumas and overcomes them in different ways, but we all need God to heal and set us free. In the human life, we have invisible chains, and often we only put a bandage or band-aid to cover the wound, without understanding the importance of healing, closing the wound, and seeking true freedom that can only be attained through Jesus.

It is impossible to heal completely if we don't take the first step, which is accepting our condition and identifying what hurt us. Accepting and recognizing that we need help is essential for healing. Forgiveness is a key piece, a necessary decision to close chapters and achieve a better life. Even our physical health improves when we forgive.

The lack of forgiveness brings serious consequences that even affect our health. We can experience heart problems, high blood pressure, fatigue, anxiety, and depression. And not only on a physical level but also on a spiritual level, the lack of forgiveness distances us from God. The word of God in Matthew 6:14 says, "For if you forgive others their trespasses, your heavenly Father will also forgive you."

In Matthew 18:21-22, Peter came to Jesus and asked, "Lord, how often will my brother sin against me, and I forgive him? As many as seven times?" And Jesus replied, "I do not say to you seven times, but seventy times seven." When we do not forgive, even our prayers are hindered and interrupted. The Bible teaches us that before offering, we must resolve any conflict, and if someone has something against you, go and ask for forgiveness.

That's how important and powerful forgiveness is. Sometimes, you will have to ask for forgiveness from those who have offended you and forgive many who haven't even come to ask for it. But it is our duty and responsibility to forgive to heal and be free.

Second Step: Identify the Root of the Wounds

We must identify the things that have hurt us to the extreme, leaving us with trauma or open wounds. What events have shaped our lives? Where did it all begin? Who hurt us? Do they still have access to us and control our emotions? Why do we behave this way (anger, frustration, lack of self-love, always defensive, overprotective, distrustful, enjoying isolation, etc.)? Is our personality tied to an event that damaged our identity?

Throughout life, the blows we face leave consequences, and often this leads us to behave in a way that traps us in repetitive cycles or constantly robs us of peace, because we build walls without even realizing it. All these things mentioned, such as anxiety, easily getting angry, etc., stem from negative experiences that remain in our subconscious; that's why it is necessary to identify the root of it all to work on those areas that affect our daily lives and those around us, without even realizing it.

In my personal experience, in order to identify those areas, it was necessary for me to sit down, reflect, and pray. I asked myself a series of questions. For example, why do I feel afraid of the dark? I remembered incidents where at night, while everything was dark, my father would take me out of my bed and bring me to his room to abuse me. My innocence associated darkness with abusc.

Another example:

For years I couldn't eat leaf cakes, I felt it would cause me to get sick to my stomach because when I was about 10 years old, I was at my paternal grandmother's house, and I loved her leafy cakes. That Sunday I must visit with my dad, my grandmother prepares food for us, I ate the cake and I go to the visiting room to rest. My dad enters the room and when I sleep, he starts abusing me sexually, I woke up from pain and fear crying and I start vomiting. Obviously, I thought the cake hurt me and for years I couldn't eat it again.

Until I was able to reflect and understand I had related the abuse to what I ate and that's why I couldn't enjoy a meal that I liked for years. In this way, I overcame it a while ago. I search for verses in the Bible that speak about fear, dread, etc. They helped me a lot in overcoming my fears and I was able to find strength in God and guidance to overcome all of this. When the enemy whispers lie that make me feel bad, I now fight back with a Bible verse that declares the opposite of Satan's lies and strengthen my mind. The Word of God is life and truth. If we don't identify the problem, we won't be able to eradicate what affects us and holds us back. It's like going to the doctor and treating the symptoms but not attacking the disease. You may feel temporary relief, but the illness will return and become stronger. For example, an infection causes fever (one of the most common symptoms). If you only take something to control the fever but don't take antibiotics for the infection, it will continue to cause harm and may even spread, affecting other areas.

When I feel attacks in my mind, I run to pray and surrender my life at His feet. Then I meditate, take notes, read the Word of God, and create a plan to overcome and strengthen myself. It will be necessary to change behavior patterns or implement new routines. But it's worth it to not ignore, but rather, recognize and seek a solution.

Step 3: Take Action and Make a Decision

It is necessary to take action, which involves seeking all the necessary help. We must not minimize the pain or the damage that has been caused. Sometimes we avoid seeking help because we feel ashamed to tell what has happened to us or fear being judged and criticized when expressing or exposing what has hurt us. We might also simply be afraid to accept that we have been left with traumas and choose to face it all alone or in silence, just as I did for many years.

It is not wrong to first turn to God in prayer, that is the first thing we should do, but it is also good to seek help. Find someone you trust and can express your feelings to, making sure that person is mature and, above all, will help you rise, heal, and draw closer to God. Recognize which areas in yourself are vulnerable and seek tools to overcome them, and above all, take refuge in God and His word. In the Bible, all the people who received a miracle acknowledged that they needed help. None of them denied their pain, frustration, or illness (condition). Just as there are physical illnesses, there are also illnesses of the soul and mind.

In every story of the Bible, we can see how they brought about their own miracle. They all acknowledged their condition and the need they had. Then they took action to provoke a miracle, a liberation, a healing, and a change in their lives. This teaches us that we must step out of the comfort zone. Constantly dwelling on the pain or the condition only leads us to feel sorry for ourselves and leaves no space for healing and restoration. Instead, when we change our victim mentality and see the lessons learned, we can grow, heal, and move forward to be a blessing to others.

Something that helped me heal was understanding that I was not responsible or guilty for what I experienced. Everyone gives what they have, and their attitude towards you reflects the internal struggles they themselves are facing and have not overcome. My struggle, your struggle, is not against those who have hurt you, it is against an enemy we all have in common, against the demons that have been assigned to destroy and delay God's plan in our lives. So, do not listen to Satan's lies, understand that you are more than a conqueror in Christ Jesus.

Forgiveness is a very powerful weapon. Many use the expression "forgiving is beneficial for you" or "forgive for yourself, not for them," and in a way, it is true! Forgiveness is for you, that is, it starts with you. But by taking that step, those around you will also receive liberation and restoration. Forgiveness brings us peace and not only benefits and frees you, but also those around you will receive that peace that you can project, and they too will be set free.

Step Towards Healing

Here are 6 steps that will help you in your healing process:

1. Recognize and acknowledge the wounds you have experienced. Allow yourself to feel the emotions associated with those wounds. This involves being honest with yourself and confronting the emotional, physical, or mental wounds you may have suffered. By acknowledging these wounds, you are recognizing their existence and the influence they have had on your life.

Remember that emotional healing takes time and patience. Each person has their own healing timeline, and it is important to respect and honor your individual process. Remember that by recognizing and acknowledging your wounds, you are taking the first step towards a healthier and fuller life. Do not be afraid to seek the help you need and to allow yourself to feel and heal.

2. Participate in prayer services to connect with God and express your pain, struggles, and need for healing. Communicate honestly and pour out your heart and soul to God. During these moments of prayer, you can speak to God with sincerity and open your heart to Him. You can share your deepest fears, worries, and frustrations, allowing your faith in God to be a source of comfort and hope.

Prayer provides you with the opportunity to seek God's guidance and strength amidst your difficulties. You can ask God to heal your emotional wounds and provide you with inner peace. By communicating with God in prayer, you can experience a sense of relief, release, and spiritual connection. Do not hesitate to honestly express your emotions to God. He is a loving and understanding Father who wants to listen to you and be present in your times of need. Prayer is a safe space where you can find comfort and receive the healing power of God.

3. Free yourself from any bitterness, resentment, or anger you may feel towards the person who hurt you. Pray to be able to forgive those who hurt you and yourself. Surrender your pain and burdens to God, trusting in His guidance and wisdom.

4. Read and reflect on God's Word that offers comfort, hope, and encouragement. It can remind you of God's love, forgiveness, and His ability to heal. Freeing yourself from any bitterness, resentment, or anger you may feel towards the person who hurt you is an essential step in your healing process. Forgiveness is an important part of this process, both for yourself and for those who have hurt you.

Recognize that forgiveness does not mean justifying or forgetting the pain you have experienced, but rather freeing yourself from its power over you. Ask God to help you heal and find peace in your heart.

Surrender your pain and burdens to God. Acknowledge that you cannot carry it all on your own and trust in God's guidance and wisdom. Allow Him to take control and have faith that He has a plan of healing for you. Remember that God is a haven and has the power to transform your pain into something beautiful.

5. Seek support in a faith-based group: Surround yourself with people who provide support, or spiritual leaders who share your beliefs. Attend Christian services, connect with others, and seek their support, guidance, and prayers in your healing process. It is also important to seek spiritual leaders who can guide you

and provide guidance in your healing process. Being surrounded by people who share your faith can provide you with a safe space where you can share your experiences and receive prayers and advice. Remember that you are not alone, and that there are people willing to accompany you on your path to healing.

6. Practice self-care: Take care of your physical, emotional, and mental well-being. Engage in activities that bring you joy, practice self-compassion, and seek professional help if needed. Trust that God desires for you to experience healing.

-Identify activities that you enjoy and that help you relax. It could be reading, exercising, pursuing a hobby, or spending time in nature. Dedicate regular time to engage in these activities and prioritize your happiness.

-Be kind to yourself and allow yourself to feel and process your emotions. Recognize that it is normal to have emotional ups and downs and give yourself permission to take care of yourself and heal. Treat yourself with love and compassion always.

-Seek professional help if needed. If you feel that your wounds are too deep or are in an emotionally challenging state to handle, consider seeking help from a Christian mental health professional who can provide you with the necessary tools and support for your healing process.

-Trust that God desires for you to experience healing: Have faith that God is with you on your healing journey. Trust that He wants to see you experience peace, tranquility, and wholeness in your life. Seek spiritual support in your relationship with God through prayer and reading the Bible.

Remember that each person is unique, and their healing process may be different. Do not compare yourself to others. Allow yourself time, patience, and love to heal and live a fulfilled life guided by God.

What is forgiveness according to the word of God?

Forgiveness is like forgiving a debt. Jesus, being holy and perfect, gave his life on the cross to forgive our debt, our sins, and through that sacrificial love and voluntary surrender, we receive restoration and eternal life. Jesus asks us to forgive those who offend us, just as He forgave our debts. He even tells us to love our enemies.

Luke 7:47 says, "Therefore, I tell you, her many sins have been forgiven—as her great love has shown. But whoever has been forgiven little loves little."

Forgiveness is based on that unconditional love that God has shown us. Without deserving it and despite failing Him daily, He sent His beloved Son to not only give His life but also to endure every affliction we face. Jesus went through all the pain and anguish as a human, undeserving of it. Now, you and I deserve many things because we are not perfect. Jesus didn't deserve it, but He did it to leave us the greatest example of forgiveness and the greatest demonstration of love. Just as God forgives us, we must forgive and love. Are we only made in His image and likeness for what is good?

We are also made to love as He loves and forgive as He did and does daily.

"For if you forgive other people when they sin against you, your heavenly Father will also forgive you. But if you do not forgive others their sins, your Father will not forgive your sins" (Matthew 6:14–15).

Matthew 18:21-35

Forgiveness restores our lives, restores broken relationships. It brings unity, peace, and understanding. It is a way to give by grace what we have received by grace. Forgiveness is like a bridge; it opens the way to love.

There are different ways of forgiving:

1. The forgiveness we receive when we offend someone, and we go to ask for forgiveness and that person grants us forgiveness.

2. The forgiveness we go and ask from the person we offended or hurt. That decision we make to go and accept our guilt and ask for forgiveness.

3. The forgiveness we give ourselves because we also harm ourselves by making bad decisions or putting ourselves in situations that lead us to be hurt or betrayed. Or we need to forgive ourselves for hurting our loved ones, like our children, because maybe we exposed them to pain and trauma. Sometimes we stray from God and sin, and it is necessary to forgive ourselves.

4. The forgiveness we release, that we give to those who hurt us but for some reason have never acknowledged

their mistake or never come to ask for forgiveness. But even so, deciding to forgive is an act of love that resembles God.

Forgiving does not mean having to fully accept those people back into your life. Forgiving means being free and setting the offender free.

Something I understood is that when I was a child or when I was in situations where I couldn't defend myself, it was not my fault or my responsibility. Those who should have protected me failed me. But now, being older and having more control over my life, I do have control. I decide what I accept in my life and who I open my heart to and give access to. Therefore, I forgive and love, but I don't allow the same thing that once marked my life to be repeated.

Now, how do I know if I have forgiven? Here are some signs that I have identified in my personal life:

- You don't judge the person who hurt you.
- You don't seek reasons for this or that.
- You can pray for them without mentioning the harm they caused you.
- When praying, you ask for their restoration and mercy.
- You don't seek revenge.

- You focus on the good qualities of that person.
- You don't wish them harm in their life.
- When talking about what happened, you can thank God because, despite everything, He took care of you, and you recognize that God has always been by your side.

Why is it important to forgive others?

Holding grudges and clinging to resentment can negatively affect our emotional well-being. Forgiveness allows us to let go of negative emotions such as anger, hatred, and resentment, which can lead to greater inner peace and happiness.

Research shows that forgiveness is a path to better mental health outcomes. When we forgive, we decrease levels of stress, anxiety, and depression. It can also improve our self-esteem and overall psychological well-being.

Forgiveness plays a crucial role in maintaining and repairing relationships. Problems are inevitable, but forgiveness allows us to move forward, rebuild trust, and foster healthier connections with others. It helps create an atmosphere of understanding, empathy, and reconciliation.

Forgiveness is a sign of personal growth and strength. It requires the ability to let go of past hurts, learn from previous situations, and choose to move forward with a positive mindset. It allows us to develop flexibility and resilience in the face of adversity.

Forgiveness is a transformative process that not only benefits us individually but also has a positive impact on our relationships and overall quality of life. Healing allows us to restore our well-being, find closure, and move forward in life with a sense of peace and healing. It is important to understand that healing is a personal journey and may take time, but it is essential for our own emotional and mental well-being.

Jesus Teaches Us to Forgive

The most beautiful and powerful story is the life of Jesus. Through Him, we learn to forgive and love even those who hurt us. Jesus was betrayed by one of his disciples. He was denied, and many of those close to him didn't believe in his mission.

He experienced everything firsthand, being God, he became man so that we, as sinners deserving eternal punishment, receive forgiveness and eternal life.

The death of Jesus on the cross was a sacrifice made to forgive the sins of humanity.

Sin separates humanity from God. It is considered as disobedience to God's will and is the root of the disappointment and spiritual separation caused by sin.

Due to the consequences of sin, humanity needs forgiveness to reconcile with God. Forgiveness of sins is seen to restore the broken relationship between God and humanity. Jesus is the Son of God who willingly took on human form. His death on the cross is seen as an expression of God's love and mercy. Jesus's death paid the price for humanity's sins, offering redemption and forgiveness to all who believe in Him.

Jesus, being innocent and without sin, bore the punishment of sin to satisfy God's justice. By accepting Jesus's sacrifice, believers receive forgiveness and are declared righteous before God.

The resurrection of Jesus from the dead shows His victory over sin and death. It offers hope to believers that they are not only forgiven but also have the promise of eternal life through faith in Jesus. Jesus has given us a great example of how we should love and forgive.

Surround Yourself with Those Who Lead You to the Miracle.

In Matthew 9:1-8, it happened one day that Jesus was teaching, and the Pharisees and teachers of the law were sitting there, having come from all the villages of Galilee, Judea, and Jerusalem. The power of the Lord was with him to heal. 18 At that moment, some people brought a paralyzed man on a mat and tried to bring him inside and place him in front of Jesus. 19 However, not finding a way to do so because of the crowd, they went up on the house and, through the roof, lowered him on the mat, placing him in the middle, in front of Jesus. 20 When Jesus saw their faith, he said to the paralyzed man, "Take heart, son; your sins are forgiven." 21 Then some of the teachers of the law said to themselves, "This man is blaspheming!" 22 Knowing their thoughts, Jesus said, "Why do you entertain evil thoughts in your hearts? 23 Which is easier: to say, 'Your sins are forgiven,' or to say, 'Get up and walk'? 24 But I want you to know that the Son of Man has authority on earth to forgive sins." So, he said to the paralyzed man, "Get up, take your mat and go home." 25 Then the man got up and went home. 26 When the crowd saw this, they were filled with awe; and they praised God, who had given such authority to man.

In this story, we see a paralyzed man who knew how to choose good friends, who pushed him to receive his miracle. They ignored his condition and did everything possible to bring him to Jesus. I want to be like those friends, to be an instrument for many to see beyond the prognosis of the situation. I want to be the one who lifts the fallen hands and helps those who have no strength to walk. Many times, God heals us, and we keep it to ourselves, but we are called to freely give what God has given us through His grace and mercy.

The wounds in our lives are meant to be used as a testimony that God restores and heals. We all have a story to share, and we can be of help to others. Spiritual people can offer the best guidance and support in the process of forgiving and healing past wounds for several reasons. They often have a deeper understanding of human nature, compassion, and the power of forgiveness. They can provide wise insights and a broader perspective on the situation, helping you overcome pain and find a path to healing.

They can share their faith and sacred beliefs, which can provide comfort and hope in difficult times. They can help you connect with God, find Him through prayer, fasting, and reading His Word, thereby strengthening your spiritual life. Furthermore, they can offer a compassionate presence, attentively listen to you, and provide guidance to assist you in the healing process.

Forgiveness can be a difficult process, but spiritual individuals may have knowledge of forgiveness practices rooted in their teachings. They can offer you techniques and prayers that help you forgive, allowing you to let go of resentment and find inner peace.

Remember that while there are people who can provide valuable support, healing is a personal journey, and it is important to find the approach and support that resonate with you. Above all, seek God's guidance.

Joseph Forgave His Brothers

In Genesis 50:14, we see the story of a young man who was betrayed and sold by his brothers. However, after going through various trials, God placed him in a position of power, and years later, he was used to help his brothers. Joseph forgave, and not only did he forgive, but he also extended his hand and showed mercy and love. Joseph forgives his brothers.

After burying Jacob, Joseph returned to Egypt with his brothers and all those who had accompanied him to their father's funeral. But now that their father had died, Joseph's brothers were fearful and said to each other, "Now Joseph will show his anger and take revenge for all the wrongs we did to him."

So, they sent a message to Joseph saying, "Before our father died, he instructed us to say to you, 'I beg you, please forgive your brothers for the wrongs they did to you.' So now, please forgive us, the servants of the God of your father." When Joseph received the message, he couldn't hold back his tears. Then his brothers came and bowed down before him, saying, "Here we are, your servants."

But Joseph replied,
"Do not be afraid. Am I in the place of God? You intended to harm me, but God intended it for good to accomplish what is now being done, the saving of many lives. So then, do not be afraid. I will provide for you and your children."

He reassured them with comforting and tender words.

Death of Joseph:

Joseph and his brothers, along with their families, continued to live in Egypt. Joseph lived to be one hundred and ten years old.

He saw three generations of descendants of Ephraim, son of Manasseh, and lived long enough to see the children of Machir, son of Manasseh, whom he considered as his own.

Joseph said to his brothers, "I am about to die, but God will surely bring you back to the land which he promised to give to Abraham, Isaac, and Jacob."

He made the Israelites swear an oath, saying, "When God visits you and brings you back, take my bones with you."

Joseph died at the age of one hundred and ten, and the Egyptians embalmed him and placed him in a sarcophagus in Egypt.

Joseph was one of the twelve sons of Jacob and enjoyed his father's favor. Out of jealousy, his brothers sold him as a slave to a caravan of Ishmaelites.

Joseph was taken to Egypt and sold as a slave to Potiphar, an Egyptian official. He worked as a slave in Potiphar's house but was falsely accused of attempted rape by Potiphar's wife, which resulted in his imprisonment.

Even in prison, Joseph maintained his integrity and interpreted the dreams of his fellow prisoners. Eventually, his gift for dream interpretation reached Pharaoh, the ruler of Egypt. Joseph correctly interpreted Pharaoh's dreams about an upcoming famine, which led to his appointment as second-in-command of Egypt.

During the famine, Joseph's brothers went to Egypt in search of food. Joseph recognized them but pretended not to know them at first. He tested their character and made them bring their younger brother, Benjamin, to Egypt.

The path to Joseph's forgiveness for his brothers is found in the book of Genesis, in chapters 42-45.

Many years after being sold as a slave by his brothers, Joseph became a powerful leader in Egypt. His brothers, unaware of his identity, came to Egypt in search of food during a famine. Joseph recognized them but did not immediately reveal his identity.

To assess whether his brothers had changed, Joseph subjected them to various tests. He accused them of being spies and imprisoned them for three days. This was the most important test to evaluate their character and see if they felt deep remorse for their past actions.

While keeping his identity hidden, Joseph was deeply moved when his brother's expressed remorse for their past actions and acknowledged their mistake. He wept and finally revealed his identity to them, showing compassion and forgiving them. Joseph assured his brothers that he had forgiven them and encouraged them not to feel upset or angry with themselves for selling him as a slave. He explained that God had a purpose in everything that had happened, turning a painful event into a greater plan for the good of many people.

There are situations where God will completely remove us, and through forgiveness, we can simply move on without having to face that situation or that person ever again. But there are others where, like Joseph, we will find ourselves in front of those who once afflicted, hurt, or betrayed us. Right at that moment, we will be tested in many areas, and it will be our decision to show God's love through how we treat those people or remain imprisoned with invisible chains.

It's not an easy thing to do, but it is powerful and brings you peace. I have been able to love so freely, I learned to be honest and transparent by genuinely forgiving. I have been able to feel that peace that surpasses all understanding, that peace that goes beyond any situation around us. God has been good, and He will always be. His mercy reached me.

Today, I can testify freely and confidently, telling you that God heals every wound. He restores, and His presence is always with you. He has blessed me with beautiful daughters, my husband's children, who have been a great blessing. I am married to Tony Mejía, a great man of God who came into my life when I least expected it. Together, we walk in this ministry and have been able to bring a message of hope and restoration.

If you so desire, I invite you to say this prayer:

Most loving Heavenly Father, in this moment, I come before Your humble presence. I acknowledge that I need Your help and healing for my heart. I desire to be set free from all resentment and pain that I have carried due to the actions of those who have hurt me.

I recognize that forgiveness is a gift You have given me, and in the same way, I want to extend it to those who have hurt me in any way. Today, I choose to forgive each one of them, and I also ask for forgiveness for my own offenses. I pray that You break any negative bond that has kept me tied to them. May forgiveness bring us peace and liberation and allow us to move forward, reflecting Your love, goodness, and compassion. In the name of Jesus, I pray. Amen

Number 1 Book of The Series Beyond My Wounds!

Another Book To Read Called From The Streets to The Altar!

The Power of Forgiveness